D1733096

# Nature's Cycles
# Day and Night

## Dana Meachen Rau

Marshall Cavendish
Benchmark
New York

Early in the morning, the sky turns pink. The sun rises in the east. Another day begins.

Early morning is called *dawn*. The air is cool and wet. *Dew* covers the grass.

Many animals wake up. Birds
start to sing. Rabbits munch
on leaves.

Kids get out of bed to start the day.

The sky brightens and turns blue. The sun seems to move higher in the sky. The moon and stars are still in the sky, too. The bright sun makes them hard to see.

Animals gather food in the day. Some animals eat berries or leaves.

Other animals hunt for food.
They sneak up on their *prey*.

Kids need food in the day.
Food gives you energy to play
and learn. You do not have to
gather or hunt. You can buy or
make your lunch!

In the middle of the day,
the bright sun heats the air.
Some animals rest in *shade*.

Other animals lay in the sun
to keep warm. Kids run around
and play outside.

Plants need the bright sunlight during the day. Their leaves use sunlight to make food. This food helps the plants grow and bloom.

In the evening, the air gets cool again. The sun starts to set in the west. The sky turns pink. It is *dusk*.

Animals find *shelter* under rocks or in trees. They may go into their underground tunnels.

A hole in a log makes a good home, too. Kids go inside their houses.

Then the night sky grows dark. Stars can be seen again. The moon looks bright.

Kids go to sleep in their beds.

Most animals rest in their shelters. Other animals wake up at night. They are *nocturnal*. They come out at night to eat.

Bats hear tiny sounds with their big ears. They use sound to catch insects at night. Owls have big eyes to see.

Lightning bugs flash to find
each other.

As the night ends, the sky gets light. The sun will soon come up. You will start another day. Nature will, too.

# Challenge Words

**dawn**—Early morning.

**dew (doo)**—Droplets of water left on grass and plants by the cool night air.

**dusk**—Early evening.

**nocturnal (nahk-TUR-nuhl)**—To be most active at night.

**prey (pray)**—Animals that are hunted by other animals.

**shade**—The shadow created when an object blocks sunlight.

**shelter**—A safe place to hide or sleep.

# Index

Page numbers in **boldface** are illustrations.

would like to thank Paula Meachen
*for her scientific guidance and expertise in reviewing this book.*

## With thanks to Nanci Vargus, Ed.D., and Beth Walker Gambro, reading consultants

Marshall Cavendish Benchmark
99 White Plains Road
Tarrytown, New York 10591-9001
www.marshallcavendish.us

Text copyright © 2010 by Marshall Cavendish Corporation

Library of Congress Cataloging-in-Publication Data

Rau, Dana Meachen, 1971–
Day and night / by Dana Meachen Rau.
p. cm. — (Bookworms. Nature's cycles)
Includes index.
Summary: "Introduces the idea that many things in the world around us are cyclical in nature and discusses how day changes to night each day"—Provided by publisher.
ISBN 978-0-7614-4094-9
1. Earth—Rotation—Juvenile literature. 2. Day—Juvenile literature. 3. Night—Juvenile literature. I. Title.
QB633.R28 2010
508—dc22
2008042512

Editor: Christina Gardeski
Publisher: Michelle Bisson
Designer: Virginia Pope
Art Director: Anahid Hamparian

Photo Research by Anne Burns Images

Cover Photo by *Corbis*/Kennan Ward

The photographs in this book are used with permission and through the courtesy of:
*Getty Images*: pp. 1, 20 Peter Litja; p. 2 Altrendo Nature; p. 5 Frank Krahmer; p. 11 Ian McCallister; p. 15 symphonie; p. 16 Rudi Sebastian; p. 19 Peter Dazeley; p. 26 Charles Melton; p. 28 Bruno Ehrs. *Peter Arnold*: p. 6 Biosphoto/Ruoso Cyril; p. 8 Biosphoto Vincent M. & Studler E.; p. 10 John Cancalosi; p. 14 Fred Bruemmer. *Photo Edit*: p. 7 Myrleen Ferguson Cate; p. 13 Dennis MacDonald; p. 23 David Young-Wolff. *Animals Animals*: p. 21 Phyllis Greenberg; p. 27 COLOR-PIC Inc. *Photo Researchers*: p. 22 Jerry Schad; p. 25 Sidney Bahrt.

Printed in Malaysia
1 3 5 6 4 2